Ignatian Spirituality

Acknowledgements

First published in 2009 by

MESSENGER
PUBLICATIONS
JESUITS *in* IRELAND

Messenger Publications,
37 Lower Leeson Street, Dublin 2
www.messenger.ie

Printed in Ireland

ISBN 978-1-872245-65-2

the JESUITS
in IRELAND
PARTNERS *in* MISSION

PRINt
IRISH
CLÓBHUAIL
in éireann

PEFC
SGS-PEFC/COC-0627

Our sincere thanks to Fr. Philip Heng SJ, whose original text "An appreciation of Ignatian Spirituality" inspired this work. Published in Singapore, a copy of his book came to our attention at a time when the Partners in Mission Office, Dublin, was looking for a similar resource. Fr. Heng generously shared his work with us and also gave us the freedom to adapt and innovate.

We would like to thank John Dardis SJ (Provincial) for supporting the publication of this book.

We would like to acknowledge the work and commitment of the team whose dedicated work resulted in this publication: Brian O'Leary SJ author of the text and articles for the present edition; John Looby SJ as Editor; the Messenger Publications Team: Triona McKee (General Manager) and Paula Nolan (Designer) for sharing both their great expertise and creativity. Thanks to my colleagues in the Jesuit Curia Office, Dublin, for their support.

For the greater part of his life, Ignatius tried to share the understanding he had of God with others. His message has great relevance today. It is fitting that this introduction to Ignatian Spirituality represents that ongoing work of sharing his insights, from East to West.

Deirdre Soffe
Director, Partners in Mission
Ireland
July 2009

A word from the Jesuit Provincial

Dear Friends,

A word of welcome to this Introductory Booklet on Ignatian Spirituality which I hope you will find helpful.

Many who encounter the work of The Society of Jesus are curious about Jesuit and Ignatian core values and beliefs. You may be working in education, spirituality or in the social justice area. You may be involved in a Jesuit school, or involved in an organisation or activity that shares a common Ignatian background or perhaps through an Order or Congregation of the Ignatian Family.

The purpose of this booklet is to introduce the Spirituality of Ignatius of Loyola and to share some of his core ideas. His perspective affirms God's Presence in all aspects of life's experience. It encourages you to recognise life's challenges and move to find a deeper meaning and value in daily life. It invites you be of service to others.

The origins of this book reflect the international nature of Ignatian Spirituality. It is an adaptation of the work of Philip Heng SJ of Singapore, whose book "An Appreciation of Ignatian Spirituality" was our inspiration and so this book reflects a collaborative undertaking between 'East and West'. My sincere thanks to him for his generosity in sharing his work and my thanks to the writers and editorial team for their work in realising this project.

I hope that in reading this book you are encouraged and supported in all that you do.

John Dardis SJ
Irish Provincial
July 2009

Contents

Introduction

Ignatian Spirituality

Its Roots in a Historical Person Ignatius of Loyola (1491-1556)

IS THERE one Christian spirituality or many? There is only one Christian spirituality, yet it expresses itself in a variety of ways. We look for our spirituality first of all in the Scriptures, particularly in the Gospels. But people respond differently to what they read in these sources. We might speak of resonance. Different biblical stories, or images, or personalities resonate more strongly in one person than in another.

I may be so moved by the compassion that I see in the person and ministry of Jesus that compassion becomes the lynchpin of my spirituality. You, on the other hand, may be captivated by the story of the rich young man. Because of this resonance you embrace a spirituality of radical simplicity. The fact that we have different responses does not mean that either of us is departing from the one Christian spirituality. However, each of us is choosing to live it out in a particular way and with a distinctive emphasis.

Over the centuries certain specially gifted women and men have experienced and responded to God in such profound ways that others have looked to them for inspiration. In some cases they have become founders of a school of spirituality, or a tradition that proves its worth simply by surviving (especially if it manages to cross geographical and cultural boundaries). Such survival, however, only happens when there is also development and growth. Tradition

is never static. Each succeeding generation contributes to and enriches the tradition through its own experience. Nevertheless, the tradition remains rooted in and identified with a historical person.

Ignatius of Loyola was one of these specially gifted friends of God. It is to him that many still look today as embodying a particular and attractive way of living the Christian faith. His life experiences speak to ours. His vision engages us. His wisdom guides us. This combination is what we call Ignatian spirituality.

Biography

Born in 1491 into a Basque family of the lower nobility Ignatius was the youngest of thirteen children. At sixteen he was well on his way to becoming a courtier, immersing himself in the culture and values of chivalry. He also involved himself in various youthful escapades. Determined to achieve the same chivalric glory he had read about in popular romances, he enthusiastically defended Pamplona against a numerically superior French army in 1521. This daring but foolhardy enterprise did not save the town and led to his being hit by a cannonball that smashed one of his legs and wounded the other.

Ignatius was brought back to his family's castle in Loyola where his recovery was long and arduous. During this time he was unexpectedly drawn to God through the only books that were available for him to read: a life of Christ, and lives of the saints. Through this reading, and by reflecting on the feelings that it aroused, he experienced a deep change within himself -- a conversion. A strong desire arose in him to serve Jesus Christ. This lead to a complete reversal of values, the worldly ones giving way to those of the Gospel. From then on desires played a central role in his evolving spirituality. He realised that desires determine the choices we make and how we act.

His new-found fascination with Jesus led to a decision to visit the Holy Land as a poor pilgrim and to pray in those places where Jesus had lived and worked. While preparing for this journey he spent almost a year as a hermit in a town called Manresa practising rigorous fasting and self-denial. He tells us in his Autobiography that here God was teaching him as a schoolmaster teaches a child. He had to learn that the spiritual life does not consist in performing great feats of asceticism (like the mighty deeds performed by knights in the romances of chivalry) but in a discerning love. Alongside desires, discerning love becomes another foundation stone for what was to come.

Also at Manresa Ignatius sought out people who were willing to

Casa Solar, Loyola, where Ignatius spent months recovering from his injury at Pamplona

speak with him about God. Initially he was seeking help for himself, but he soon discovered that these conversations were also helpful to others. They became the basis of the Spiritual Exercises* that he began to write down at this time. He experienced a growing desire *aiudar a las almas* (to help souls) and the Exercises became his main way of fulfilling this desire. Now he had added an apostolic dimension to his spirituality: to help souls becomes a core value (today we speak of helping the person). All this was happening while Ignatius was still a layman.

After returning from the Holy Land he began formal studies at the age of thirty-three. Beginning in Barcelona, and continuing in the

The Holy Land: Jerusalem

Universities of Alcala and Salamanca, he moved eventually to the University of Paris in 1528. Here for eight years he gave himself to philosophy and theology. Although never an academic he performed well in his studies. But his motivation was always pastoral. His studies were a means enabling him to be more effective in his dealings with people.

In Paris he won over to his dreams a small group of young men, the best known being Francis Xavier and Pierre Favre. In 1535, during a Mass celebrated in Montmartre, they pledged themselves to live in chastity and poverty, and together to travel to the Holy Land. When their plans to sail across the Mediterranean were frustrated by war between Venice and the Turks, the companions went to Rome to place themselves at the disposal of the Pope. By now they were ordained priests. Discerning that they should form a new religious order they presented a formal petition to Pope Paul III who approved the foundation of the Society of Jesus (later known as Jesuits) in 1540. Ignatius was elected as the Society's first Superior General.

After so many journeys Ignatius spent his last sixteen years in Rome. From there he guided the development of the rapidly growing order, overseeing missions in Europe, Asia and South America. Much of his time was given to a voluminous correspondence (nearly 7000 letters are extant) that testifies to his dedication, flexibility and moral strength. Although no longer a traveller he continued

* See page 47

the most important journey of all, his inner journey that centred on his search for God and God's will. During this time he was graced with a profound mystical prayer. All of this was accompanied by increasingly bad health. He died on the morning of 31 July 1556. The Society had by then grown to about 1,000 members.

There have been many images of Ignatius over the centuries since his death. The four most significant are the following:

Ignatius the Pilgrim

Soldier-saint. This originates from his early involvement in the culture of chivalry and his military exploits at Pamplona. Along with the image of the Society of Jesus as the "light cavalry" or the "shock troops" of the Roman Catholic Church, it suited the militant spirit of the Counter-Reformation.

Skilled organiser. This image stems mostly from an appreciation of the Constitutions that Ignatius wrote for the Jesuit order. These are widely regarded as a managerial masterpiece. Whether one regards Ignatius as Spirit-filled or Machiavellian in their composition depends on one's point of view!

Mystic. This is a favoured image of Ignatius among his followers today. It derives from his mystical experiences, especially those in Manresa and in Rome. It stresses that his relationship with God is the core of what makes him admirable, as well as being the source of his teaching and other achievements.

Pilgrim. However, Ignatius' own self-image remained that of the pilgrim. This is how he referred to himself in the Autobiography that he dictated near the end of his life.

In the following pages we shall be exploring more deeply the life here outlined so as to distil from it a spirituality relevant for people of our time.

Jesuit Spirituality ~ Ignatian Spirituality: the same or different?

THIS BOOK is entitled Ignatian Spirituality. Is this simply another name for Jesuit spirituality? Are the terms Jesuit and Ignatian synonymous? Or can we distinguish between the two? And if we can, does the distinction matter?

To answer these questions it will help to revisit Ignatius' life. We have seen that up to their priestly ordination in 1537, he and his companions were laymen. As students in Paris they were living a spirituality that was rooted in the Scriptures and moulded by the experience of the Spiritual Exercises. During this period they continually sought to discover the will of God regarding their future orientation and work. In this discernment they engaged in fervent prayer, called on all their human resources, and waited on God. By the Feast of Our Lady's Assumption in 1534 they felt ready to commit themselves to the

Ignatius presenting the Constitutions of the Society of Jesus for approval to Pope Paul III, who approved the Order on September 27, 1540

service of God by making vows of poverty and chastity. They also vowed to go on pilgrimage to the Holy Land where Christ had lived and died. But, knowing the threat to Christendom from the Turks, they added a rider: If they were unable to get to the Holy Land they would journey instead to Rome and make themselves available to the Pope, Christ's Vicar on earth.

Their foresight proved to be prudent, but also providential. When the time came for their intended voyage across the Mediterranean, war between Venice and the Turks prevented all pilgrim ships from sailing. So the rider came into effect and the companions, all now ordained, headed for Rome. The Pope gladly accepted their offer of availability and soon made it clear that he intended to act on it – by beginning to send them on missions. The first few were within Italy but the companions knew that eventually they would be dispersed far and wide. They realised that they would have to deal with this new situation. So they entered into a further period of discernment, known as the "Deliberation of the First Fathers", at the end of which they decided to strengthen their already existing union by forming a new religious order.

In this way the "Friends in the Lord" became the Company or Society of Jesus, and were soon known as Jesuits. This name originated as a term of abuse but eventually gained acceptance even among Jesuits themselves. Ignatius was elected the first Superior General and was commissioned to write the Constitutions of the order. These give expression to a specifically Jesuit spirituality which leads men to live under vows in the service of God and the Church. Jesuits make the

of a special obedience to the Pope "concerning missions" (a replication of the offering of the First Companions in 1538). It is worth quoting the Constitutions on this point.

To avoid erring in the path of the Lord, they (the First Companions) made that promise or vow in order that His Holiness might distribute them for greater glory to God. They did this in conformity with their intention to travel throughout the world and, when they could not find the desired spiritual fruit in one region, to pass on to another and another, ever intent on seeking the greater glory of God our Lord and the greater aid of souls (Const. 605).

Is the distinction between Ignatian and Jesuit spirituality becoming clearer? The First Companions lived Ignatian spirituality up to the time when they became a religious order. We might say that they were living out of the Spiritual Exercises. For most of that time they were laymen, for a short period they were secular priests. However, once they made religious vows in the Society of Jesus they began to live Jesuit spirituality. They did not cease to live out of the Spiritual Exercises but these were now supplemented by the Jesuit Constitutions. Neither did they cease to be Ignatian, but they were now Ignatian in a manner that was appropriate for vowed, apostolic religious.

What of today? The Second Vatican Council spoke of the universal call to holiness, of how everyone is called into union with God in Christ. Ignatian spirituality is at the service of this teaching, this reality. All who desire to do so may live and grow in holiness through the practice of Ignatian spirituality. Whether you are male or female, young or old, healthy or ill, married or single, working or unemployed, Ignatian spirituality enables you to find God in the concrete circumstances of your life. All Christians hear this universal call to holiness, but every individual also hears a uniquely personal call. Each then will discover how Ignatian spirituality "fits" their particular lifestyle, or using a different metaphor, how Ignatian spirituality moulds itself to the shape of that lifestyle.

Finally, it is tempting to look for the distinction between Ignatian and Jesuit spirituality by reference to Jesuit mission. While there is some value in this approach, it is no longer fully satisfactory since so many other priests, religious and lay people are now associated with that mission. Jesuits are not alone in being involved in many so-called "Jesuit ministries". (Looking to differences of lifestyle, as above, leads to a better understanding of the distinction). We now use a variety of different terms in referring to those who share the apostolic task with us Jesuits: e.g. partners in mission, co-workers, collaborators, associates, and so forth. These terms affirm that now we all share in the one mission. I end with an apt quotation from GC35:

As the Holy Father affirmed our ministry and mission, saying to us "The Church needs you", we must turn to our collaborators in mission and say, with gratitude and affection, that the call we have received is a call shared by us together (Decree 6, 3).

For further reflections on the above themes, see "Jesuit Mission: Corporate and Global" (pages 14-19).

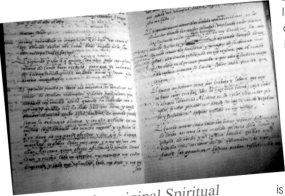

Pages from the original Spiritual Exercises with notations by Ignatius

The Manresa Experience: Mystical Gifts

Manresa today

*F*resh from his initial conversion at Loyola, Ignatius, as we have already seen, spent eleven months in Manresa (1522-1523). He was on his way to the Holy Land as a pilgrim and initially intended to spend no more than a couple of days in the town. But something held him there and his stay turned out to be transformative in his life. From his Autobiography we can distinguish three different phases of contrasting experiences:

1. "Days of light" (April to May) during which he was gifted with peace and joy. This was a kind of honeymoon period, often associated with the immediate aftermath of a conversion. In his naivety he thought that it would last forever!

2. "Days of darkness" (May to end of July) during which he struggled with doubts and other kinds of desolation, culminating in a devastating battle with scruples. These were so severe that he even considered suicide. He was being brought down to earth.

3. "Days of glory" (August to mid-February) during which God enlightened him in a series of mystical experiences. These were so profound that he would often refer back to them in later life, especially at times of serious decision-making.

What were these mystical experiences through which Ignatius was enlightened? He speaks initially of five: an understanding of the Trinity, of how God created the world, of how Christ is present in the Eucharist, a vision of the humanity of Christ, and a vision of Our Lady. We notice immediately that these experiences are deeply theological. He is being "given to understand" the basics of Christian faith. He ends his account with these striking words:

These things that he saw at that time fortified him and gave such great support to his faith that many times he thought to himself: if there were no Scriptures to teach us these matters of faith, he would still resolve to die for them on the basis of what he had seen (Aut. 29).

It is important to recognise that his enlightenment was not about abstract truths but about a personal God who is in relationship with us. God was revealing himself through these "visions", enabling Ignatius to enter into the mystery of the divine: The Trinity (God is a community), Creation (all that God made is good), Eucharist (God shares his life with us), Christ's humanity (Jesus, although God, is like us in all things except sin), Our Lady (Mary models our relationship with her Son and with the Father).

However, these experiences were surpassed by another known as the "great enlightenment". It took place on the banks of the river Cardoner that flows through Manresa. In his own words:

He was once on his way, out of devotion, to a church a little more than a mile from Manresa, which I think was called Saint Paul. The road followed the path of the river and he was taken up with his devotions; he sat down for a while facing the river flowing far below him. As he sat there the eyes of his understanding were opened and though he saw no vision he understood and perceived many things, numerous spiritual things as well as matters touching on faith and learning, and this was with an elucidation so bright that all these things seemed new to him. He cannot expound in detail what he then understood, for they were many things, but he can state that he received such a lucidity in understanding that during the course of his entire life – now having passed his sixty-second year – if he were to gather all the helps he received from God and everything he knew, and add them together, he does not think they would add up to all that he received on that one occasion (Aut. 30).

Like his comment after describing the five earlier experiences, this account ends with a similarly remarkable claim. The Cardoner experience was without doubt the highpoint of his enlightenment by God. The content of this enlightenment is more difficult to identify. He speaks of understanding "numerous spiritual things as well as matters touching on faith and learning". But what were they? He does not specify. Probably (though by no means certainly) he was not being taught new truths but was seeing familiar ones in a more penetrating light (they seemed new to him). And since he speaks

Ignatius the Mystic

of the Cardoner experience immediately after his description of the earlier visions, it is at least conceivable that he received *inter alia* a still deeper understanding of the Trinity, Creation, Eucharist, humanity of Christ, and Our Lady. But there was another crucial aspect to this experience by the Cardoner.

Unusual, if not unique, in this portrayal of a mystical experience is the incorporation of "learning" in its content (from the word he uses it is clear that this refers to secular learning). Its inclusion indicates that he grasped within the experience the inter-relatedness of truth – bringing together matters of the spirit, of faith, and of secular learning. One of the early Jesuits wrote that at the Cardoner Ignatius saw "the guiding principles and causes of all things". He saw how all things, secular as well as sacred, human as well as divine, had their source and origin in the creator God. All this is implied by the word "inter-relatedness". This reading of the Autobiography helps us to understand, however obscurely, how the Cardoner experience bore fruit in Ignatius as the gift of discernment. It became for him the touchstone for all his future decision-making.

Grasping the inter-relatedness of truth also allowed Ignatius to develop a spirituality that may broadly be called humanistic. I say broadly because the words "humanism" or "humanistic" are problematical when applied to Ignatius. He was certainly not a humanist in the modern sense where the term has been hijacked by atheistic secular humanism. But neither was he a humanist in any way that would place the human person rather than God at the centre of the universe. For Ignatius God is always the ultimate reference point for all of reality. So I use the word "humanism" of Ignatius simply to indicate his reverence for the whole of creation, his valuing of the human person with all his or her gifts, talents, and creativity, his conviction that there is a need to foster the human as well as being open to the divine. This led eventually to the emergence of the apostolate of education within the early Society of Jesus,

The image of Ignatius the mystic may never be as concrete or tangible as that of the soldier-saint, or the skilled organiser, or even the pilgrim. Yet our reflections on what happened at the Cardoner clearly show his mystical experience as anything but ethereal or otherworldly. Ignatius is far from being some blithe spirit floating above the drama of life. While he was certainly drawn into the mystery of the divine his Cardoner experience also engaged him more deeply in the mystery of the human. From then on his thinking and decision-making always sought to bring together these two polarities – the divine and the human, all to the greater glory of God.

Jesuit Mission: Corporate and Global

Baptism: Wah Yan College, Hong Kong. 24 December, 1933. Fr Gallagher SJ, centre. Top row, third from left, A. Fei, errand boy; top row, right, A. Koon Shang, games boy; bottom row, left, A. Chung, carpenter. The other three in the photo are the Godparents. The Jesuits first went to Hong Kong in 1930.

Hong Kong, 25 August, 1935. Father Jung SJ preaching to the people at the sea shore.

WHEN Ignatius had his conversion experience, first at Loyola and later at Manresa, he saw himself as a sinner before God. His response was to undertake a regime of extreme penance in an attempt to atone for his sins. It was only gradually that he came to realise that a life of service to others (*aiudar a las almas*) was more pleasing to God than a life of asceticism alone. He broke out of a self-centred spirituality into one that embraced other people. In the light of his success in helping others, especially through spiritual conversation, he considered the future. He came to realise that by acting alone he could reach a very small number of people. However, if he had a committed group around him their service could be more widespread and effective. Consequently he made efforts to gather companions, first but with little success in Spain, then more successfully in Paris. We refer to the group around Ignatius from that time onwards as "the first companions".

The dynamic that was going on in Ignatius can be described as a move from the personal to the corporate. From the I of his conversion (called by name) he was being drawn to the WE of the group (called into community). He was no longer relating to God or to others simply as the individual, Ignatius of Loyola, but as part of a "body", a community of persons who shared his spirituality – a spirituality that had an apostolic vision at its core. The early development of this corporate sense in Paris came to its fullness some years later in Rome when the Society of Jesus came into being. This embracing of the corporate does not entail the loss of, still less the destruction of, the personal. Individual identities in all their uniqueness and integrity are retained, but they now exist in relationship with the corporate entity of which they are a part. Indeed they can be expected to flourish within the body.

This development in Ignatius is mirrored in the link between the Spiritual Exercises and the Jesuit Constitutions. The Exercises enable

Walter O'Connor SJ, March, 1951. 'Maize at Chikuni Mission', Zambia. He writes: "This snap gives you a better idea of the height of our maize – at least three to four feet higher than myself. The boys are beginning to enjoy a good feed! Notice that two of them are wearing rosaries – a practice we are trying to introduce here. This snap was taken on a boiling hot day in late March."

an individual to undergo a conversion experience and find meaning in life through a serious response to the will of God. They cater to the needs of the I. The Constitutions, on the other hand, focus on what Ignatius calls "the body of the Society taken as a whole", elaborating a corporate spirituality at the service of a corporate mission. They may be said to cater to the needs of the WE. Yet the I and the WE are interwoven since the Constitutions presume that they are being lived by people who have made and prayerfully assimilated the Spiritual Exercises.

John Guiney SJ amongst the displaced in Khartoum, 2006.

We have seen that Ignatius sought out companions precisely because he wanted to reach more people in service. After the founding of the Jesuits his/their apostolic horizon continued to expand. The sixteenth century was the era of the great voyages of discovery. As "new" countries were opened up to Europeans Ignatius was not the only churchman who saw enormous potential for evangelisation. He seized these opportunities with enthusiasm (e.g. in sending Francis Xavier to the Indies). When he writes in the Constitutions about the Jesuit choice of ministries, his foundational criterion is that "One should keep in mind the greater service of God and the more universal good". This is accompanied by other criteria such as responding to areas of greater need and/or going where there is likelihood of reaping greater fruit. We could describe his criteria as always expansive, always reaching for the magis (the greater). They ensure that the horizon and desires of the Society and its members are never constricted.

Perhaps the most striking expression of this outlook, this spirituality, is his statement that "The more universal the good is, the more is it divine". This is the conviction that has energised Jesuits over the centuries, encouraging risk and adventure, movement to the frontiers (wherever and whatever they may be at any particular time), and courage to dialogue with unfamiliar cultures and new ideas. Addressing the delegates to the 35th General Congregation (2008) Pope Benedict XVI honed in on this tradition and affirmed it in these words:

> As my Predecessors have said to you on various occasions, the Church needs you, relies on you and continues to turn to you with trust, particularly to reach those physical and spiritual places which others do not reach or have difficulty in reaching.

He goes on to quote his predecessor, Paul VI, as he addressed the delegates to the 32nd General Congregation (1974):

Phnom Penh 2009: child on a rubbish dump.

> Wherever in the Church, even in the most difficult and extreme fields, at the crossroads of ideologies, in the front line of social conflict, there has been and there is confrontation between the burning exigencies of human beings and the perennial message of the Gospel, here also there have been, and there are, Jesuits.

Many are surprised to learn of the prohibition in the Constitutions on Jesuits taking responsibility for the care of parishes. While this restriction has now been lifted it is enlightening to reflect on the reasons Ignatius had for his prohibition. For him the pastoral care of parishes was one of the great needs in the Church of his time. Yet he saw that such work would tie down Jesuits, limit their mobility and availability, restrict their freedom to respond to new situations, new crises, new opportunities anywhere in the world. He wanted Jesuits to live "with one foot in the air" which they could not do if they were accountable to a particular localised group of people (parishioners). The principle of universality had to be protected.

A principle, of course, needs to be applied. Each generation of Jesuits is called to discern how universality is to be lived in the

Upendo Unit of St. Joseph the Worker Primary School, Nairobi, Kenya. January, 2009. Upendo unit is for HIV orphans. Frs Kyalo, John Guiney and Lamullen SJ are the priests of the parish.

historical and cultural environment of its time. How to keep the more universal good in mind, indeed use it as a basic criterion, when making choices that are necessarily limited? From the point of view of spirituality the end result of such discernment is less significant than the process of discernment itself. Ultimately it is not what we do that is most important but why we do it. Spirituality is about the why. When we look at ministries that Jesuits are involved in or committed to today, these should be understood as emerging from the discernment of the Society, especially that of recent General Congregations. In the richer formulations of such decisions we find interwoven a combination of the spiritual and the practical. For example, in the key document of GC34 (1995) entitled 'Servants of Christ's Mission' we read:

Today we realise clearly:
No service of faith without
    Promotion of justice
    Entry into cultures
    Openness to other religious experiences
No promotion of justice without
    Communicating faith
    Transforming cultures
    Collaboration with other traditions
No inculturation without
    Communicating faith with others
    Dialogue with other traditions
    Commitment to justice
No dialogue without
    Sharing faith with others
    Evaluating cultures
    Concern for justice

A woman suffering from leprosy, with her child, in Uganda.

This helpful formulation of the interplay between the four key commitments of the contemporary Society – the service of faith, the promotion of justice, engagement with culture, and interfaith dialogue – remains valid. The more recent GC35 attempted a similar schematisation by using the lens of "right relationships". It spoke of three areas in which reconciliation was needed and to which we were invited to contribute: reconciliation with God, with one another, with creation. This last is a new element since GC34, arising from the urgency of care for the earth and the universe.

John Guiney and Murt Curry from the Irish Jesuit Mission Office with Bishop Macram Max Gassis of Sudan on the Bishop's visit to Ireland.

One of the positive effects of globalisation has been to make possible the living out of this focus on the "more universal" in ways undreamed of in Ignatius' time. Today Jesuits are able to think and plan more internationally. Traditionally governance in the Society was built on Province structures, with Province boundaries normally corresponding to those of national or regional territories. In today's world such Province boundaries are becoming porous as Jesuits seek inter-Province collaboration, and the creation of new cross-Province initiatives.

An example close to home is an agreement between the Irish, British, Dutch and North Belgian Provinces to adopt a number of apostolic priorities to guide their common way forward. In the form of questions these include:

- How can faith confront secularism?
- How can we help young people find God?
- How can we show the Gospel's credibility by work for justice?

Decisions on priorities such as these, like the decrees of General Congregations, are the result of much prayerful discernment, both individual and corporate. They in turn call for even further discernment. It is an ongoing process, rooted in the teaching of Ignatius in the Spiritual Exercises and the Constitutions.

Finally and crucially, Jesuits no longer see themselves as alone in their mission. They are committed to collaboration with others in all that they do in (what Ignatius called) the "vineyard of the Lord". Decree 2 of the 35th General Congregation puts it strongly:

In such changing circumstances, our responsibility as Jesuits to collaborate at multiple levels has become an imperative. Thus our Provinces must work ever more together. So also must we work with others: religious men and women of other communities; lay persons; members of ecclesial movements; people who share our values but not our beliefs; in short, all people of good will.

An acceptance of the "ethos" of a Jesuit institution allows collaboration to be sincere and effectual. However, for those who wish, Jesuits are more than happy to share their spirituality and to offer programmes and other supports to nourish its growth. Those who accept this offer learn to live Ignatian spirituality, not only in their collaborative endeavours, but in their family and social lives as well. Something new is coming into being whose future holds out great hope for this global, multicultural, apostolic body.

We end with another quotation from the 35th General Congregation, this time in Decree 6. It sums up much of what we have been saying:

Charles Searson SJ on a return visit in 2007 to Canisius High School in Zambia, Central Africa. Canisius Secondary School was started in 1949 by Father Max Prokoph SJ and run for many years by the Irish Jesuits. It is currently run by a team of lay teachers and Jesuits from all over the world, the majority of whom are Zambians. It was the first Catholic secondary school in what was then Northern Rhodesia and second in the whole country. By 1964, the year of Zambian Independence, it had educated many of the leaders of the country. This is still true to date. The school motto "Moniti meliora sequamur" "Having been taught, let us follow the better things" although from Virgil's Aeneid fits well with the "magis" of Ignatian Spirituality.

In his day, St. Ignatius gave shelter to the homeless of Rome, cared for prostitutes, and established homes for orphans. He sought collaborators and with them established organisations and networks to continue these and many other forms of service. To respond today to the pressing needs of our complex and fragile world, many hands are surely needed. Collaboration in mission is the way we respond to this situation. It expresses our true identity as members of the Church, the complementarity of our diverse calls to holiness, our mutual responsibility for the mission of Christ, our desire to join people of good will in the service of the human family, and the coming of the Kingdom of God. It is a grace given to us in this moment, one consistent with our Jesuit way of proceeding.

Key to Collage

1. Slí Eile volunteers working with the children in Mother Teresa Hospice, Lusaka, Zambia.
2. Dr Mary Redmond, who chaired a public seminar in 2008 titled *Women In Prison: The Need for a Critical Review*, run by the Jesuit Centre for Faith and Justice (JCFJ).
3. Jesuit Refugee Service (JRS) Western Balkans, formally JRS Bosnia-Croatia, started in 1993 following the war in the Balkans. As well as their office in Kosovo, the JRS has offices in Bosnia and Herzegovina, Croatia and the former Yugoslav Republic of Macedonia.
4. Fr J Brereton SJ and Fr B Bradley SJ with a young student reading at the special Mass in honour of Fr. James Cullen SJ at Clongowes Wood College SJ, Kildare.
5. Clongowes' Students in attendance at the special Mass to honour Fr James Cullen SJ.
6. The Ballymun Gospel Choir.
7. The School Boards meet in Kildare.

8. IHS-AMDG is the Jesuit Emblem. IHS are the first three letters of the Greek word for Jesus, IHSOUS. In Latin, the letters stand for *Jesus Hominum Salvator*, 'Jesus, saviour of man'. AMDG, *Ad Maiorem Dei Gloriam*, translates 'To the Greater Glory of God'.
9. Overcoming obstacles: children from St Declan's school in Dublin.
10. Coláiste Iognáid: Shane Conneely, Cpt Sn Rugby, with President Mary McAleese, during the President's visit to Coláiste Iognáid on March 4, 2009.
11. The Crescent College Comprehensive SJ in Limerick is celebrating 150 years this year. This is a specially commissioned logo to mark the occasion.
12. Emerson Burke Murphy, a student from Gonzaga College, with friends in Zambia.
13. Slí Eile's Debbie Moore with the children of St Annie's Jesuit Parish, Kingston, Jamaica.

14. Gonzaga College SJ, Dublin: on the rugby pitch.
15. Gerry O'Hanlon SJ at the launch of the book, *So You Can't Forgive?* by Brian Lennon SJ, a Jesuit based in Armagh.
16. Scholastic Maurice King – with Zebra! Maurice is studying philosophy at Heathrop in London.
17. Clongowes Wood College SJ: warming up. This photo, and many great photographs on the Clongowes website, was taken by the art teacher, David Nelson. www.clongowes.com
18. Ashley Evans SJ with his students after Mass on Palm Sunday 2009. Ashley is based in Cambodia.
19. Richard Leonard SJ.
20. The Belvedere College annual Christmas sleepout to raise funds for the homeless.
21. Manresa Jesuit Centre of Spirituality, Dublin. www.manresa.ie

Windows into Ignatian Spirituality

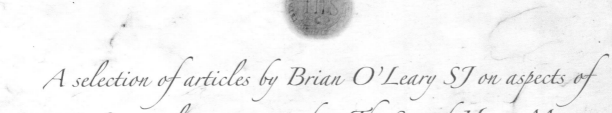

A selection of articles by Brian O'Leary SJ on aspects of
Ignatian Spirituality as appeared in The Sacred Heart Messenger.

These articles are best read one at a time, slowly, taking time to reflect after each one.

Ignatius the Pilgrim

IGNATIUS OF Loyola was canonised on 12th March 1622, along with his friend, Francis Xavier, and two other well-known saints, Philip Neri and Teresa of Avila. These four outstanding Christians witnessed to the vibrancy of renewal in the Church of the sixteenth century. They gave expression to the Church's holiness in different and creative ways. Three of the four were born in what is now modern

Ignatius of Loyola and Francis Xavier

Spain. All lived in a century of great change. The Renaissance was fostering developments in art and culture, and was transforming the approach to education throughout Europe. The Protestant Reformations (there was more than one) introduced new ideas into theology and spirituality, and challenged the authority of the Roman Church. The voyages of discovery led to a vast expanding of people's imaginative horizons, brought immense wealth back to Europe from the recently conquered lands, and opened a new era of missionary work for the Church.

We have learned to pay more attention to the historical context of saints' lives than we may have done in the past. The turbulence of the sixteenth century affected Ignatius' thinking, his choices, his spirituality, and therefore his holiness. He would have been a different person, a different saint, if he had lived in the ninth or nineteenth century. But under God's providence he walked this earth at a particular time (not any time), in a specific historical era (not some other era),

meeting certain people (and not others). It was in these concrete circumstances that he sought and found God, that he grew in holiness. We cannot turn Ignatius into a twenty-first century person. We cannot simply imitate him in every aspect of his life. Likewise, knowing historical facts about Ignatius will not of itself contribute much to our own growth. If we want to be helped we need to get inside his experience, so far as that is possible. We need to discover how God dealt with him.

This need was expressed very clearly by one of Ignatius' friends in 1551. This man, Jerome Nadal, was one of a number of Jesuits who wanted Ignatius to tell the story of his life. But he wanted it told in a particular way. This is how he reports on his approach to Ignatius: "I begged the Father to be kind enough to tell us how the Lord had guided him from the beginning of his conversion". He was not asking for an autobiography in the ordinary meaning of that word. In such an autobiography the focus is on the person telling their story, what they did, said, saw, achieved, suffered, and so forth. Ignatius was being asked to recount what God did in him, how God taught, led, guided, challenged, loved him since his conversion in Loyola in 1521. The focus was to be on God. Readers would learn about the ways of God more than the ways of Ignatius Loyola. This was to be its importance.

Ignatius was curiously hesitant about telling

this story and kept putting off the effort. This was partly due to ill health, partly to the pressure of urgent business, and partly to a lingering fear of vainglory. But perhaps most of all it was an example of a reticence, quite typical of him, about speaking of his inner experiences of God. However, he eventually dictated an account to another Jesuit, Gonzalves da Camara, and this relatively short work gives us a precious insight into God's ways

Philip Neri
and Teresa of Avila

of dealing with him. In spite of its not being an autobiography, it is most frequently referred to in English as the Autobiography (as I will continue to do). But other titles, also in use, are perhaps more accurate, such as A Pilgrim's Journey, Original Testament, or simply Reminiscences. But whatever this account is called it is one of our main sources for getting inside the experience of Ignatius and learning from it.

It can surprise readers who come across this work for the first time that Ignatius narrates his story in the third person. Is this another instance of his reticence? Using the third person allows him to create a certain distance from the experiences of God that he is describing. There is also less danger of falling into vainglory if he is not referring to 'I' and 'me' on every page! But more importantly, he gives this third person a name, 'the pilgrim'. In doing this he is offering his readers a key to unlock and enter the narrative. His story will be about movement, about journeys. God will be seen to lead him along many paths. Some of these paths are quite literally the roads of Europe that bring him to Montserrat, Manresa, Barcelona, Alcala, Salamanca, Paris, Venice and Rome. But sometimes the paths are metaphorical, referring to an inner journey that over years will have Ignatius change, develop, and grow into a person totally

in love with God.

Neither the starting-point of the outer or the inner journey gives any clue as to where it will end. Convalescing in his family's castle in Loyola Ignatius had no idea that the final years of his life would be spent in Rome. The same can be said about his inner journey. It begins with the opening sentence of the Autobiography: "Until the age of twenty-six he was a man given up to the vanities of the world, and his chief delight used to be in the exercise of arms, with a great and vain desire to gain honour". It ends at the time of narrating his story when he can say: "He was always growing in devotion, i.e. in facility in finding God, and now more than ever in his whole life. And every time and hour he wanted to find God, he found him". The Autobiography is mainly the story of that inner journey, of how God led him from being an ambitious, boisterous knight, filled with dreams of chivalry, to becoming a person whose only desire was "to praise, reverence and serve God our Lord".

All Christians are pilgrims. We are on a journey like Abraham who "set out, not knowing where he was going" (Hebrews 11:8). Abraham is praised for his faith, which in this context is synonymous with trust. He trusted the One who had called him. He did not need to know the destination. It was enough that God was with him. So too with Ignatius who trusted that God would not desert him, abandon him, or allow him to go too far astray. Both his story and that of Abraham invite us to a similar trust. Life will always bring changes, gains and losses, clarity and confusion. Through it all we are encouraged to leave ourselves in the hands of God, to allow him to write our personal history.

Learning from Daydreams

THE EARLY part of Ignatius Loyola's life is probably better known than his last years in Rome. He was wounded while leading the defence of the citadel of Pamplona against an invading French army. That stubborn, heroic but futile display of bravery remains readily in the memory. Similarly the scene where he lies on his bed in the castle of Loyola, recovering from his wounds and subsequent surgery, also captures the imagination. We may well have gone through periods of convalescence ourselves and so can empathise with the boredom he felt. Ignatius did not have a radio at his side or a television monitor over his bed. He tried to relieve the tedium (and the pain) by asking for what most appealed to his taste in reading, romances of chivalry. But none could be found in the castle. It was apparently not a household where much reading was done. All that came to hand was a book of Lives of the Saints, and the Life of Christ by a medieval Carthusian, Ludolph of Saxony.

What followed at Loyola is often called his conversion. It might be more correct to say the beginning of his conversion. This was to be a gradual process, continuing through his later experiences at Manresa and beyond. The word 'conversion' can sometimes be misleading if it is interpreted too narrowly (as it often is) to refer to moral behaviour only. But morality is only one dimension of conversion, and perhaps not the most profound. Underlying it there is a conversion, a turning to God. Having made that turn a person sees everything in a new way. Remember that Native American saying, 'Where you plant your feet determines what you see'. The person who has turned to God now has a new and wider horizon. Beauty reveals itself in unexpected places. Virtue begins to seem attractive. Personal priorities begin to be revised. New decisions are called for and made.

This is the kind of experience that Ignatius had as he convalesced. It was, of course, grace at work. But what way did grace 'get through' to Ignatius? We tend, perhaps, to think of God speaking to our reason, our understanding, our conscience, or drawing us through our feelings. Both reason and feelings came to be involved in Ignatius' conversion but the whole process began with his imagination, his ability to daydream! The lack of books telling stories of knights and ladies, thrilling adventures and great deeds, loyalty to a king and love of a fair maiden did not prevent Ignatius from imagining such scenarios. This was the imaginative world in which he normally lived. Of course, he was always the hero! He tells us in the Autobiography that he spent many hours in such daydreams, and in particular "imagining what he was to do in the service of a certain lady: the means he would take so as to be able to reach the country where she was, the witty love poems, the words he would say to her, the deeds of arms he would do in her service".

When Ignatius turned to the Life of Christ and the Lives of the Saints his vivid imagination was still at play. He asked himself, "How would it be if I did this that St Francis did, and this that St Dominic did?" He was daydreaming, playing with an alternative set of possibilities to those of being the chivalrous knight. Yet he was still thinking like a knight. He was

Triumph of
St. Ignatius
of Loyola, by
Andrea Pozzo.
Painted on
the ceiling of
Sant'Ignazio,
Rome, Italy

focusing, not on the inner life of Christ and the saints, not on the values they lived by, but on their great deeds. Soon the possibility ("How would it be if...?") became an imperative, "St Francis did this so I must do it; St Dominic did this so I must do it". It was an impulsive, immature response, of no great spiritual depth, but it was where Ignatius was at that time. And it was enough to allow God to lead him a bit further and continue teaching him.

Like many energetic people who have been forced into inactivity by illness or convalescence Ignatius was becoming more reflective. He was growing more aware of the oscillating feelings that he was experiencing. In a particular way he was noticing changes of mood in relation to his reading and his daydreaming. Both imagining himself as the romantic, swashbuckling knight, and imagining himself performing great deeds for God (mostly imitating the penitential practices of the saints) brought him great delight. He really enjoyed playing the hero! But now he began to notice a difference in the aftermath of the two kinds of daydreaming. Whenever he stopped musing about knightly honour and adventure "he would find himself dry and discontented". But whenever he had been engaged with thoughts about the great deeds he would do for God "he would remain content and happy even after having left them aside". Noticing all this did not immediately bring understanding "until one time when his eyes were opened a little, and he began to marvel at this difference in kind and to reflect on it ... and little by little coming to know the difference in kind of spirits that were stirring: the one from the devil, and the other from God".

The word 'spirit' in this context can be puzzling for some people. It refers to movements within us, sometimes accompanied by a lot of emotion, that influence us in some way. We find ourselves drawn towards some person, idea, or course of action. This brings with it feelings of enthusiasm, elation, desire, love, and so on. Or we find ourselves repelled by some person, idea, or course of action. This, on the contrary, brings with it feelings of distaste, revulsion, fear, antagonism, and so on. When we notice what is going on there are two questions we can ask. The first is: Where is this spirit, this movement, leading to? If I follow through on the direction of this movement will I find myself coming nearer to God? Or will I be moving away from God? The second question is: Where has this spirit, this movement, come from? Has it come from God or from some source that is not God? The two questions go together. A movement that is bringing me towards God is clearly one that has come from God. Whereas a movement that is leading me away from God is obviously coming from a source other than God.

This was, in fairly simple terms, what Ignatius learned at Loyola. It was the first step in his understanding of discernment. This theological word, sometimes overused or misunderstood nowadays, refers to the art of distinguishing one kind of spirit or movement from another. Discernment is at the heart of what we now call Ignatian spirituality. As with Ignatius it begins with awareness, with noticing, with paying attention to all our inner experiences. Then come the questioning and the interpretation. Ultimately we are asking "Where is God in all of this?" "How is God communicating with me here?" We do not need extraordinary experiences in order to discern. God speaks through our quite mundane human experiences of mind, heart and imagination. All that is needed on our side is attentiveness and prayerful reflection.

If you are not accustomed to living with this level of awareness, perhaps you can learn from Ignatius' experience. You could begin by practising on your own daydreams!

Three Things I Pray

THE SEVENTIES' hit musical *Godspel* presented the story of Jesus in a lively, contemporary idiom. This resonated with a whole generation, many of whom, although nominally Christian, had drifted away from organised religion. One of the show's best-loved songs was the infectious "Day by Day", based on a prayer by a medieval English bishop, St. Richard of Chichester (1197-1253). In its original and fuller form this reads:

> *Thanks be to you, my Lord Jesus Christ*
> *For all the benefits you have given me,*
> *For all the pains and insults you have borne*
>   *for me.*
> *O most merciful Redeemer, Friend, and*
>   *Brother,*
> *May I know you more clearly,*
> *Love you more dearly,*
> *Follow you more nearly,*
> *Day by day. Amen.*

As audiences at Godspel swayed to the rhythm and sang along with the music, they were frequently being drawn into a spiritual experience. They were getting in touch with some of their deepest desires. As they expressed in words their (perhaps suppressed) yearning for a close relationship with Jesus ("Three things I pray"), they were reviving the religious dimension of their lives.

Was Ignatius familiar with this prayer of Richard of Chichester? We do not know. But whether he was or not, he certainly came close to duplicating its final lines in the Spiritual Exercises. In introducing the kind of prayer that we know today as gospel contemplation he writes: "I ask for what I want: here I ask for interior knowledge of the Lord who became human for me so that I may better love and follow him". The wording is more sober, and it lacks the rhyme and rhythm of Richard's prayer or the Godspel song. But the "Three things I pray" are essentially the same: to know, to love,

Page from Ludolph de Saxony's 'Life of Christ'

to follow Christ. However, Ignatius has added a word of great importance, the adjective "interior" to describe the knowledge of Christ that is desired. We need to return to this.

Ignatius' approach to gospel contemplation is a version of *lectio divina*, the venerable monastic way of prayer that has spread well beyond monastic circles in our own day. What is characteristic of the Ignatian approach, however, is his encouraging of the use of the imagination. He suggests an imaginative entering into a gospel scene or event (what the tradition called a "mystery" of Christ's life), so that we become totally present to it. We gaze at the persons, we listen to what they are saying, we observe what they are doing, we speak with Jesus or with some other person or persons in the scene about what is happening and what this is evoking in us.

We might even 'take part' in the scene (for example, having our feet washed by Jesus at the Last Supper, or helping to place the body of Jesus in the tomb). We can do this either by remaining ourselves, or by (imaginatively) becoming one of the gospel characters (for example Peter or Mary of Magdala), or by (imaginatively) becoming an 'extra' (for example, another blind beggar in a scene of healing). There is no one way of becoming part of a gospel event; whatever way suits us is best.

All of this is aimed at drawing us into the full reality of what is happening, inserting us deeply into the event or 'mystery' we are contemplating. It is a way of ensuring that the knowledge of Christ that we are asking for will be truly 'interior'. What then is meant by interior knowledge? We might clarify what we mean by contrasting such interior (or intimate) knowledge of a person with a knowledge that is objective, intellectual, clinical. We are touching on the difference between knowing a person and knowing about a person. The latter can be attained through gathering facts and processing information. It is the result of research and study. But in gospel contemplation we are seeking the kind of knowledge that a wife may have of her husband, or a father of his child, or a lover of her beloved. Such knowledge only comes from two people being together over a period of time, perhaps many years, interacting with each other, sharing life's experiences.

So in gospel contemplation we stay with Jesus as he is born, grows, relates, works, travels, teaches, enjoys, suffers, and so forth. We desire to get inside his experience, not just to know the external details of his life, but to know him from the inside out. Since such intimate knowledge of another person is always pure gift, we need to keep asking Jesus to be gracious and to reveal himself. "'Come', my heart says, 'seek his face!' Your face, Lord, do I seek. Do not hide your face from me" (Ps. 27:8-9). With this desire we keep developing a contemplative attitude towards Christ, allowing him to reveal himself as he really is, and not as what we might want him to be.

Ignatius had first learned about this kind of prayer from Ludolph of Saxony's *Life of Christ* that he had read during his convalescence at Loyola. In the Preface to this work the author writes about entering gospel scenes or events:

> Hear and see these things being narrated, as though you were hearing with your own ears and seeing with your own eyes, for these things are most sweet to him who thinks on them with desire, and even more so to him who tastes them. And though many of these are narrated as past events, you must meditate them all as though they were happening in the present moment, because in this way you will certainly taste a greater sweetness. Read then of what has been done as though they were happening now. Bring before your eyes past actions as though they were present. Then you will feel how full of wisdom and delight they are.

All relationships that have any depth involve mutuality. As we desire that Jesus reveal himself to us, so too we reveal ourselves to Jesus. We share with him our own lives, our struggles and successes, the darkness of our doubts and the brightness of our hopes. We allow him to get to know us, to have an interior knowledge of us, at the same time as we receive an interior knowledge of him. Our human need to be known lies very deep within us. It complements our desire to know the other person.

This mutuality brings a wholeness to the loving relationship that we long for with Christ.

Light and Darkness

Vision of St Ignatius, Cathedral of St. Barbara, Kutna Hora, Czech Republic

PEOPLE WHO have undergone a deep conversion, whether moral or spiritual, tend initially to experience a period of unruffled consolation. To friends and observers it may even seem that they are "on a high". This is what happened to Ignatius at the beginning of his stay in Manresa. In the Autobiography he says, "Up to this time he continued undisturbed in the same interior state of great and constant joy without knowing anything about internal spiritual matters". As he looks back he realises that the joy or consolation of that period of his life was accompanied by much ignorance. He is not referring to ignorance of book-learning but to lack of experience of the inner life. Such experience was not long in coming.

The first disturbance that shook his composure

was a temptation to discouragement, an agitated questioning of his ability to persevere in his good intentions. "Perceiving that this was the voice of the enemy, he likewise interiorly answered and with great courage: 'O, you wretch! Can you promise me one hour of life?' Thus he overcame the temptation and remained tranquil". However, dealing well with this experience of inner turmoil was only the beginning. Ignatius continues his story:

> After the above-mentioned temptation, he began to feel notable changes in his soul. Sometimes he was so dejected that he found no enjoyment in the prayers he recited, not even in attending Mass, nor in any other form of prayer. Sometimes the exact opposite happened to him, and so suddenly that it seemed he had stripped away all sadness and desolation, just as one strips a cloak from another's shoulder. He was astonished at these changes, which he had never before experienced, and said to himself: "What kind of a new life is this that we are now beginning?"

Does any of this seem familiar? Have you noticed in your own life a similar pattern of alternating moods in the context of your beliefs? Have you undergone such a shift of feeling in relation to your faith in God, or your efforts to pray, or attending Mass – elation and deflation, warmth and coldness, comfort and boredom? If so, have you too reacted with surprise, bewilderment, confusion? But what Ignatius is describing, and what many good people also experience, is quite normal. At the time the new convert did not know this. In his ignorance Ignatius thought that he should always be in consolation. Simply turn to God, pray, do penance, lead a good life, and you will always be at peace. Not so!

> My child, when you come to serve the Lord, prepare yourself for testing. Set your heart right and be steadfast, and do not be

impetuous in time of calamity (Sir. 2:1-2).

Being impetuous would involve surrendering to the natural urge to give up when we are getting no satisfaction from our religious practice. Being steadfast involves the opposite, that is, continuing to trust God, to pray and go to Mass in spite of the aridity, boredom, or even pain of the experience.

Ignatius tends to use the word "desolation" to cover all kinds of emotional disturbance, or the absence of any emotional response at all, in our relationship with God. But, having learned from his own experience, he does not see desolation in wholly negative terms, as though it were a spiritual catastrophe. He urges us to remain faithful, to refuse to give in to the desolation, and to rely on God to lead us out of the darkness in his own time. If we take that approach desolation can become an opportunity for an increase in self-knowledge, a purifying of our motives, and growth in our love of God. Ignatius wrote in his Rules for the Discernment of Spirits: "When we are in desolation we should think that the Lord has left us to our own powers in order to test us (*see the quotation from Sirach above*), so that we may prove ourselves by resisting the various agitations and temptations of the enemy". We see here how the mature Ignatius, in contrast to the immature convert of his early days at Manresa, has come to understand the nature of desolation and is no longer surprised or frightened by it. It is simply a normal episode in the spiritual life, to be dealt with firmly, and indeed as calmly as we can.

At the heart of all desolation there lies a sense that God is either distant or wholly absent, that God has withdrawn his love from us and abandoned us. This is often accompanied by a reactive tendency on our part to blame ourselves for what is happening. Why would God be treating us like this unless we had done something wrong? It must be our fault! God must be punishing us! Such thoughts are almost always untrue and unhelpful, and need to be resolutely set aside. Otherwise we get sucked even deeper into the desolation, into our feelings of isolation, abandonment, and helplessness.

This is why the next part of the previous quotation from Ignatius' Rules is so important: "For we can do this (i.e. resist the desolation) with God's help, which always remains available, even if we do not clearly perceive it". Another way of expressing this teaching is that a felt absence of God is not the same as a real absence. We may not feel that God is with us but that does not mean that God (and God's help) is really not with us. Indeed, faith assures us that God is always present to us, even if in desolation it is a faith that cannot see, that is forced to live in darkness. We may be encouraged by the words of Jesus, although spoken in a different context, to doubting Thomas, "Blessed are those who have not seen and yet have come to believe" (Jn. 20:29).

Once we come to accept that it is quite normal for periods of desolation to alternate with periods of consolation (when we feel comfort, joy, and ease in our relationship with God), we experience a great freedom. We are no longer overly dependent on the state of our feelings. We learn to pray out of sadness, darkness, and inner dryness as much as out of joy, lightness of spirit, and bubbling enthusiasm. Ignatius offers us the reassurance that when darkness comes from deep within us, or from a succession of difficult events in our lives, we can still cling in faith to the Lord's words,

"*Can a woman forget her nursing child,*

or show no compassion for the child of her
  womb?
Even these may forget,
yet I will not forget you" (Is. 49:15).

We can then be as content to pray like Jacob wrestling all through the night with the angel – from which he came away wounded in the thigh (Gen. 32:22-32) – as to pray like Mary, Martha's sister, who sat quietly at Jesus' feet listening to him speak (Lk. 10:38-42). This pattern of alternating

Ignatius holding the Constitutions

moods is the reality of the "new life" that opened up for Ignatius at Manresa. It is a life that is rich in contrasts, comforting and challenging, through all of which God leads us more deeply into his own divine life.

Freedom for Discernment

THE SPIRITUAL Exercises of Saint Ignatius offer a way of coming to a good decision on a major issue in a person's life. For example, a person may be facing a choice about getting married, or entering religious life, or changing career, or volunteering for development work overseas. These are difficult decisions, not to be taken lightly, and they will affect many people besides the one making the choice. A Christian will want to make such a decision in line with Christ's teaching and example, or in other words by using the criteria of gospel values. More bluntly, a Christian will not simply be asking "What do I want to do?" but "What does God want me to do?" He or she will desire to be able to say, like Jesus, "My food is to do the will of him who sent me, and to complete his work" (John 4:34).

The question about what God wants of me can be experienced as oppressive and threatening unless I know in my heart and in my gut that God loves me unconditionally. "Because you are precious in my sight, and honoured, and I love you" (Isaiah 43:4). "For surely I know the plans I have for you, says the Lord, plans for your welfare and not for harm, to give you a future with hope" (Jeremiah 29:11). What resonance do these words have for me? If I hear them as addressed to me personally, and can accept them as an assurance that the God who loves me will be with me, then I can proceed with confidence. I will know that what God wants of me is not only for my good, but will turn out to coincide with my own deepest desires.

Yet even with such assurance decision making is often a process marked by fluctuations of mood and even by struggle. Why might this be? It is because once I begin to face the prospect of a major decision in my life, one that will require a radical change and a deep personal commitment, all kinds of feelings begin to surface. Some of them will carry me along happily enough, such as attraction, energy, generosity, enthusiasm, and hope. But others will disturb me and hold me back, such as anxiety, fear, apathy, self-doubt, and anger. How I deal with these fluctuations, this emotional roller coaster, is at the heart of what is called discernment. All such feelings can bring self-awareness and self-knowledge, but they can also reveal the direction in which God is leading me.

Furthermore, by acknowledging and facing these conflicting feelings I am enabled to grow in freedom. The freedom at issue here is not the kind that safeguards me from outside pressures or coercion (such as political freedom, or freedom of worship). It is an inner freedom, a spiritual freedom, that allows me to see myself and the world around me objectively, to respond to what I see lovingly and magnanimously, and to make my decision in the light of God's invitation and encouragement. Much of the Spiritual Exercises revolve around this issue of spiritual freedom, suggesting ways of attaining it under God's grace. In the earlier parts of the Exercises the emphasis is more on a freedom from sin, the roots of sin, disorder, addictions, selfishness, and the baleful influence of those cultural values that are opposed to the gospel.

But soon the emphasis is placed on a freedom for service, discipleship, witness, loving relationships, and whatever I am discovering that God is asking of me. Do I want only what God wants? This is the test of my level of freedom.

The difficulty that I have in making important decisions can be caused by many factors. Sometimes it is due to the complexity of my life situation; at others it may be due to the number of imponderables that face me as I look to the future. Sometimes it seems that God is absent or silent, and not supplying me with any guidance; at others the problem is that the options in front of me all seem equally attractive, good and promising. But in numerous cases the difficulty is simply that I do not have sufficient inner freedom to make a good decision. It may not be immediately apparent that this is the block I am experiencing. I may not be conscious of what is really going on within me. Lack of inner freedom often

has a way of concealing itself, or of seeming to be something else. But when my lack of freedom becomes clear, then I will need to focus my desires and prayer on growing into freedom. Once I have attained sufficient freedom it can be surprising how many things fall into place. Where matters formerly seemed confused they are now clear; where I had seemed trapped in apathy I now feel energised; where I was full of fear I am now ready to decide with boldness.

Against this background it is interesting to read how Ignatius described his Spiritual Exercises. They are "every way of preparing and disposing one's soul to rid herself of all disordered attachments, so that once rid of them one might seek and find the divine will in regard to the disposition of one's life for the good of the soul" (Exx. 1). Or in another paragraph, "Spiritual Exercises having as their purpose the overcoming of self and the ordering of one's life on the basis of a decision made in freedom from any ill-ordered attachment" (Exx. 23). The language and tone are those of a sixteenth-century writer, but the content of Ignatius' words resonates with our contemporary experience of struggling with decision making. The Spiritual Exercises continue to offer us a way forward, to help us grow into freedom as mature Christian disciples, and to use this freedom in the service of God and of God's people, *ad maiorem Dei gloriam*.

To the Greater Glory

LOOK AT the façade of any Jesuit church, or gaze around its interior, and you will almost certainly find the inscription AMDG. You will also find it on many buildings used for Jesuit ministries (such as schools and retreat houses), as well as on books, magazines, letterheads, and so on. AMDG stands for the Latin words *ad maiorem Dei gloriam*, or in English "To the greater glory of God". This phrase is often considered as the Jesuit motto. It was a favourite expression of Ignatius. But it is by no means exclusive to Jesuits. Pope John Paul II, whenever he was writing, printed the letters AMDG on the top left of every page. The composer Johann Sebastian Bach, a Protestant, was known to write them on his finished works, either above or below his own name. AMDG is a way of saying that we want whatever we do, think, say or write to be ultimately for God and in some mysterious way to give glory to God.

Glory is an extremely rich and multi-layered concept, itself laden with mystery. In the Bible the phrase "the glory of God" is sometimes a synonym for God himself. In Ezechiel the glory of God first abandons, then later returns to the Temple. Here the glory of God stands for a manifestation of God's presence. While humans can never see the Deity, they may behold his glory when it appears. This understanding is also associated with the pillar of cloud by day and the pillar of fire by night in Exodus (during the journey of the Israelites across the desert). Or in less extraordinary form, "The heavens are telling the glory of God" (Ps. 19:1).

When we speak of giving glory to God we are using the term in a different but related way. Glory is not something that God does not have, so that we then give it to him. If God were to lack anything he would not be God! It may help to underline two aspects of "giving glory" – an acknowledgement of the supreme greatness of God, and an urge to praise him for his greatness. In one of the weekday Prefaces in the Mass we say, "You have no need of our praise, yet our desire to praise you is itself your gift". This is close to saying, "You have no need that we should give you glory, yet our desire to give you glory is itself your gift". We can acknowledge and praise God's greatness only because he makes it possible for us to do so. It is not God's need but ours that is at issue.

So giving God glory has more to do with us – with our faith, our inner attitudes, and even our feelings towards God. It has to do with our sense of the mystery of God. Are we in touch with all of this? When we say "Glory be to the Father, and to the Son, and to the Holy Spirit", are our feelings in harmony with our words? When we sing "Glory to God in the highest", are our spirits lifted through this joyful proclamation? Is glory a word that embraces our sentiments of reverence, adoration, wonder, awe, and creaturehood when we raise our hearts and minds to God? Does it signify our gratitude and release our desire to praise? Or do we say the word without any feeling? Has the word become meaningless? Has the salt lost its taste?

In 1609 a young woman of twenty-four was arranging her hair before a mirror in her lodgings near St. Clement's Churchyard on The Strand in London when she had an extraordinary experience. For many years Mary Ward had been trying to discover how God wanted her to live her life. In this mystical experience, which came unexpectedly in the course of a mundane activity, God showed her that her current plans to enter the Carmelite Order were not what he desired,

...but some other thing was determined for me, without all comparison more to the glory of God ... I did not see what the assured good thing would be, but the glory of God which was to come through it, showed itself inexplicably and so abundantly as to fill my soul in such a way that I remained for a good space without feeling or hearing anything but the sound 'GLORY, GLORY, GLORY' (Autobiography).

Mary Ward goes undercover by dressing as a servant to reach her aunt and bring her to the Catholic faith.

Here God is promising Mary that he has another call, another gift in mind for her. This as yet unnamed vocation will give God greater glory than would her entry into Carmel. As this promise is being given she is taken out of herself and so filled with God that the word 'GLORY' in all its intensity resonates at the depth of her being. Like Abraham she is being empowered to "set out, not knowing where (s)he was going" (Heb. 11:8). Later, after further divine enlightenment, she was to found an Ignatian congregation for women. Its two branches are known today as the Congregation of Jesus (CJ) and the Institute of the Blessed Virgin Mary (IBVM/Loreto).

But Mary Ward already had something of the Ignatian spirit through her desire to give herself to what was "without comparison more to the glory of God". The AMDG motto is not just about glory but greater glory. Ignatius frequently uses this comparative form of speech. It is an expression of his magnanimity, his chivalric spirit, never satisfied with the good but always seeking the better. When suggesting criteria by which Jesuits are to choose which ministries to undertake, he writes:

One should keep the greater service of God and the more universal good before his eyes...that part of the vineyard ought to be chosen which has greater need... where the greater fruit will probably be reaped.

This habitual way of thinking in comparative terms, of desiring God's greater service and greater glory, will always draw us beyond where we are now. It is never easy but can bring the best out of us. It invites us to be willing to leave our comfort zone, to be challenged and stretched by new possibilities and fresh horizons. It brings Ignatian people to the frontiers of evangelisation.

In these reflections we have taken two approaches to the motto AMDG. The first raised questions about the feelings that accompany our use of the word "glory" in worship and prayer. I suspect that the feelings that would spontaneously call forth a cry of "Glory to God!" in Ignatius and Mary Ward came more readily to them than to us. This has something to do with the way our images

Mary quells a mutiny on board by invoking her patron St. James. Mary afterwards declared that she had never sought any favour from God through the intercession of this great prince of heaven without it being granted to her. This image, and the picture on previous page, are from: 'Life of Mary Ward', told in fifty 17th century paintings that hang in the IBVM convent in Augsburg, Germany.

of God have changed. In earlier times the holiness, majesty, awesomeness, and "otherness" of God were more evident to believers and touched them deeply. In our day we have a diminished sensibility to these qualities in God. This is our loss. We might even say that we have domesticated God!

Our second approach recognised that giving glory to God is not only a matter of feelings and of words. In the Spiritual Exercises Ignatius teaches that "Love ought to find its expression in deeds more than in words". We can say the same about giving God glory. For Ignatius doing good, being of service to others, helping wherever we can, being committed to justice – all this gives glory to God. His is a spirituality of active involvement in our world. We are encouraged to be "people for others". It is easy to see why the words "glory" and "service" are almost synonyms for Ignatius. The greater service is the greater glory, and vice versa. God is glorified in any service we give to God, to the Church, to other people. Such service acknowledges God's existence and manifests God's presence.

We might encourage one another by offering the blessing that Ignatius wrote at the end of one of his letters: "May you always persevere, growing in God's service, with much honour and glory to him and great benefit to his holy Church".

The Call to Interiority

'INTO GREAT Silence", Philip Groening's 2005 documentary on life in the Grande Chartreuse, has been described as one of the most mesmerising and poetic chronicles of spirituality ever created. Indeed it is more a contemplation or meditation than a documentary. Jesuits, along with others living an Ignatian spirituality, experienced a profound resonance in viewing this almost entirely wordless film. Some returned to view (contemplate!) it more than once. Can we explain this paradox? How could people dedicated to a life and active ministry in the world be so moved by a portrayal of monks whose call is to withdraw from that world? What is it that lay at the heart of this strange affinity? I suggest that it lies in the value that both Ignatian and Carthusian spirituality place on interiority. The Carthusian cell (a two-storey cottage with an enclosed garden) symbolises this interiority in a physical way. The monk lives in his cell in order to cultivate interiority and so find God. Ignatian people carry their "cell" in their heart, entering it in recollection and prayer. They too cultivate interiority but in the very different context of being inserted into the world.

The Jesuit Cardinal Martini, formerly Archbishop of Milan, recently wrote about Ignatius. Having referred to the dramatic times in which he lived, he asks what message Ignatius might have for the third millennium, and answers as follows:

> I think there is one especially salient message Ignatius can give us: the great value of interiority. I mean by this everything that has to do with the sphere of the heart, of deep intentionality, of decisions made from within.

Interiority is precisely the word that I too would use in responding to this question. Self-knowledge, purifying the heart, the inner journey, finding one's centre, the still point – these and other similar ideas and images have always been present in the Christian spiritual tradition. They echo but go beyond the older Greek philosophical teaching attributed to Socrates: "The unreflected life is not worth living". In the Christian experience all of this is linked with prayer – not just saying prayers but praying from the heart, praying at all times, really becoming people of prayer. One might adapt Socrates and say, "The prayer-less life is not worth living".

The argument for interiority today is not simply that it has been a constant part of the Christian spiritual tradition. It is also that interiority is the antidote to much that is insidiously destructive in our contemporary society. The spread of materialism, the speed of life, the pressures of competition, the seductiveness of consumerism, the threat to our sense of security generated by economic recession, the mind-controlling power of the mass media, the intrusiveness of advertising – these and other influences mould our way of living. Busyness replaces reflectiveness, anxiety replaces serenity, and the craving for instant gratification replaces thoughtful attention to long-term goals, especially those of the spirit. Even the quality of our most precious relationships is frequently put at risk. We are drawn to live superficially, on the surface of things, losing touch with our deeper and more real selves.

We may not have succumbed to all these

dangers, yet few would deny that we experience a struggle to "live out of our centre" and to act in accordance with our deepest desires. These desires may even remain hidden or buried, lost from consciousness. "What do you really want?" (as opposed to "What would you like?") is often a surprisingly difficult question to answer.

We may also be deceived by the apparent good. Secular values can be disguised in religious clothing. Take the example of activism. Some people go from one good deed to another, always on the move, always involved in some activity. They never pause and reflect; they never put aside time simply to be by themselves, enjoying the beauties of God's creation or the uplifting sounds of great music. Their activity has become compulsive. It is no longer freely chosen. They would not know what to do if they stopped. In fact they are terrified of being still, and maybe even more of silence.

Ignatius was convinced that good people are not likely to be deceived or led astray by blatant or gross temptations. They have to be lured by an idea that either appears to be good, or really is good but not appropriate at this time. He writes:

> It is a mark of the evil spirit to assume the appearance of an angel of light. He begins by suggesting thoughts that are suited to a devout soul, and ends by suggesting his own. For example, he will suggest holy and pious thoughts that are wholly in conformity with the sanctity of the soul. Afterwards, he will endeavour little by little to end by drawing the soul into his hidden snares and evil designs.

This quotation from the Rules for Discernment deals with a situation where both the temptation itself and the ways of dealing with it are very subtle. But the basic presupposition is clear. We recognise the temptation for what it is, we discover what is really happening, only if we are practising interiority. Without self-awareness, and a sensitivity to how God is working in us, we will be deceived. In our example, we will be drawn into a compulsive activism because it seems to be good – unless we can reflect, enter our inner space where God speaks, and learn what God really wants of us at this time. It may be to act, or it may be not to act. But in either case prayerful reflectiveness will lead to a free decision on our part.

The practice that Ignatius offers us to grow in interiority is the Consciousness Examen. An older generation knew this as the Examination of Conscience, where we looked back on the day (or some other period of time) and sought to discover where and how we had offended God. This led to a prayer that expressed sorrow and a purpose of amendment (Act of Contrition). This exercise served many people well. However, a closer look at the teaching in the Spiritual Exercises has revealed the possibility of an expanded approach. The shift from the word "conscience" to "consciousness" allows us to see the difference.

Conscience is the moral sense that we possess enabling us to distinguish right from wrong. The Examination of Conscience tended to focus on sin and the occasions of sin, on failure and on our need to be forgiven. This is not left aside in the Consciousness Examen but it becomes part of something bigger. Focusing on consciousness opens up the many ways in which we can become sensitive to the presence or absence of God in our lives. So as we allow the day to pass before our inner eyes we try to become aware of the situations, the events, the people in whom we found God, and those other situations, events and people in whom it was difficult to find him. We can pause in thanksgiving when God's presence was palpable, and pause in regret when we missed, ignored or did not appreciate that presence.

In activating our conscience we mainly make use of our reasoning (enlightened by faith). Consciousness, however, brings us also into the

area of affectivity, our inner world of feelings and emotions. We learn to notice these changing moods and movements, and to take them seriously. Since conscience deals with sin and the occasions of sin the focus is on actions that are freely carried out. Consciousness, on the other hand, includes a range of spontaneous, "non-free" movements, emotional reactions to people and situations over which we have no control. God is as much in this swirling, unpredictable mix of spontaneities as in our most rational thinking. Once we recognise this we are on the way to discerning and interpreting how God is leading us and guiding our lives. It all begins when we answer the call to interiority.

Some *Characteristics* of *Ignatian Spirituality* and testimonies to their impact in daily life

i First Characteristic: True Self-worth

Our culture has spawned a raft of teachings and techniques that claim to bring us to self-fulfilment and inner happiness. Those who offer such services have obviously recognised a human need crying out to be met, a void within the spirit waiting to be filled. In spite of superficial signs of self-satisfaction and even arrogance, people today often have a lower self-esteem than they pretend.

As a consequence many of us look to *work* to give meaning to our lives. When introduced to a stranger we tend to state what we do rather than reveal who we are. If we are not worth much, why let another person know?

God's view of us is very different. "So God created humankind in his image, in the image of God he created them; male and female he created them" (Genesis 1:27). He saw that everything that he had made was "very good" – very worthwhile. Even sin cannot destroy that basic goodness.

Furthermore, since we are good we are loveable and God reacts to us accordingly. "Because you are precious in my sight, and honoured, and I love you" (Isaiah 43:4). Even in our human interactions another person's love is what most affirms our worth. How much more does God's love make us realise how unique, precious and loveable we are!

This is the truth about ourselves. On this foundation we build our lives with confidence. We also become God's ambassadors, bringing the Good News to the people of our time.

When I wanted to join the Jesuits what caught my attention about the Jesuit charism was its universal availability – that is, to serve God's people in the Church and in the world by serving any person, any place and any time, for God's Greater Glory. I am more convinced now than ever before of how powerful and prophetic such a charism is to our present secular world and the Church's needs.

After being a Jesuit for 26 years, I have also come to realise more fully that the more we are able to love God whose Spirit is present within us, the more fully we discover the "beauty" of ourselves. This "beauty" is the inner sense of our true self-worth that comes from being so personally loved by God. The more we are able to affirm this reality the freer we are to grow into what God wants us to be and become – God's dream for us! This "dream" unfolds itself in surprising and challenging ways, but always grounded in the concrete realities of our daily living.

St Ignatius' insights of "Finding God in all things" – and in ourselves – provide us with a world view of life that is particularly needed today. Secular values distort who we truly are because God is presented as irrelevant and unimportant to our daily living. God's love is real, personal and powerfully present within us – to have the grace to sense this is to possess the "precious pearl" of the field that Jesus speaks of in the Gospel.

Fr Philip Heng SJ
(Parish Priest of Jesuit Church of St Ignatius, Singapore)
Author of *An Appreciation of Ignatian Spirituality*

ii Second Characteristic: God Labouring Within Us

At the end of the Spiritual Exercises Ignatius offers a "Contemplation to Attain the Love of God". In it he suggests different ways in which we can become aware of God in our lives. He first presents God as a "Giver of Gifts" – gifts ranging from our existence, our relationships and our personal talents to our redemption by Christ and God's gift of himself to us. In recognising that "all is gift" we are moved to respond with love.

Next he invites us to see God dwelling in all his creatures – including me, in whom he is present as in a temple. God is not distant or aloof; he is closer to each of us than we are to ourselves. Then Ignatius points out that this is not a passive presence, but that God *labours for us* in all of creation, and (I would add) *labours in us* for all of creation. This dynamic image is foundational to Ignatian spirituality.

The saga of creation did not end when God rested on the seventh day. We might even say that God left creation unfinished and gave humanity the responsibility to bring it to completion. All human activity – scientific research, developing earth's resources, enhancing our world through culture, promoting justice, etc. – is a work of co-creation. We are co-operating with God who *dwells actively* (labours) within us and within all that he has made.

Ignatius was not afraid of engagement with the world (as if it might contaminate the Christian). On the contrary, he saw such engagement in all its possible dimensions as holy, sanctifying. Through it we come into union with God.

'It's all about me' – This is an attitude that I carry with me, that the success or failure of a task I'm involved with is dependent on my will and my control of the situation. I have identified this to be unhealthy for me and view it as a part of me that needs to be 'fixed'. However, if I try to change myself, it is almost always harsh and judgemental; God's way is always tender – a constant but patient invitation to allow love, not fear, to be my guiding principle. When I try to live out of love it results in a change of focus; life becomes more about service than success, relationship rather than return. When God calls and I answer, it moves from being 'all about me' to 'Christ with me, Christ before me, Christ behind me and Christ within me'.

Edel Roddy
Project Worker, Dublin and Galway,
Slí Eile Jesuit Centre for Young Adults.

iii Third Characteristic: A Compassionate and Merciful God

At the head of each chapter of the Koran there is the dedication, "In the Name of God, the Compassionate, the Merciful". This title implicitly acknowledges our human need to be accepted and forgiven. We stand before God as sinners, knowing that we are helpless to free ourselves from our guilt. We need to hear our God saying, "I am He who blots out your transgressions for my own sake, and I will not remember your sins" (Isaiah 43:25).

Many people are reluctant to face up to their sinfulness. They may want to cling to their former way of life. Or their image of God may be that of a stern judge or an avenging ruler. In the Spiritual Exercises Ignatius invites us to discover what it is to be a forgiven sinner. This turns out to be a deeply consoling experience, one that reveals the unconditional love of God. We learn that we no longer need to earn God's forgiveness; it is freely given.

God's compassion extends beyond our personal sins. Wherever there are people suffering, or in pain, or treated unjustly, there is the God who identifies with them and desires to relieve them of their burdens. Christ's Passion opens up this mystery for us. As the English mystic, Caryll Houselander, wrote, "We cannot shed a tear, but that tear has already blinded the eyes of Christ. We cannot be without tears, but that constriction of the heart has constricted His heart" (This War is the Passion).

In our own pain – physical, psychological, or spiritual – we receive God's compassionate love; then in "com-passion" we offer our own love to others.

Ignatian Spirituality is central to the life of my Religious Congregation, and hence, to my own personal life and mission. As I reflect on God's mercy and compassion, an image comes to mind. In contemplating the Incarnation, St. Ignatius asks us to turn our eyes towards the Trinity and see how the Three Divine Persons look down on our world, in its darkness, brokenness and confusion, and decide to enter into our human family so that we might experience his love and be saved.

Working with the J.U.S.T team in Ballymun I am aware that there is still much darkness and brokenness in people's lives. I am part of their struggle towards a more human quality of life, but I also carry within my heart a deep peace and confidence, knowing that the Risen Jesus is still in our midst, working with us and drawing us into the Father's love.

While respecting the journey of each person, I feel called to make God's compassion, mercy and justice real for people who suffer in so many ways from poverty and injustice. The support given by the J.U.S.T. project, enabling people to continue their education and enhance the quality of their lives is, for me, a means of being with Christ in his saving mission.

Sr Teresa Brogan
Sister of Marie Auxiliatrice
Jesuit University Support and Training
(J.U.S.T.) in Ballymun

Fourth Characteristic: Sharing in Christ's Mission

We see in the gospels that Jesus' relationship with his Abba/Father meant everything to him. His personal sense of identity, as well as the choices he made throughout his life, were based on this relationship. He saw himself as one sent by the Father. Indeed his identity and his mission are one. To be Son is To be sent is To be on mission.

Consider the texts: "My food is to do the will of him who sent me, and to complete his work" (Jn. 4:34), "I have come down from heaven, not to do my own will, but the will of him who sent me" (Jn. 6:38).

The primary meaning that Ignatius gives the word "mission" is similar: actively "to send" or passively "to be sent". Only secondarily does it signify a content – what one is sent to do. As with Jesus, so with all Christians. We share in Christ's mission because through baptism we share in his Sonship. For us also To be sons/daughters is To be sent is To be on mission.

Through discernment we discover the specifics of our mission. We first contemplate the gospels to learn the mind and values of Christ. We then acknowledge our talents and abilities. Finally, we consider the signs of the times. "The joys and hopes, the grief and anguish of the people of our time, especially of those who are poor or afflicted, are the joys and hopes, the grief and anguish of the followers of Christ as well" (Vat. II, "The Church in the Modern World"). Relying of these three "resources" we ask for enlightenment and the courage to decide and to act.

I work in a prison with guys that are serving long sentences for different crimes. This means I am challenged to enter a space that's very uncertain and uncomfortable at times for me. So I rely on an attitude of trust.

Yet another experience moves me when I leave the prison. I feel energised from this dialogue we share. It is one that moves me to feel closer to God. The line "we are each used as his instruments to draw others closer to God" calls me to wonder who is serving whom? Which of us is the instrument in our work? This experience brings me closer to understanding my own salvation, by sharing dialogue with society's so-called 'outcasts and undesirables'. Even in my best moment of giving, I am also receiving. My understanding of that makes me feel alive and aware of the source of my life. This is what I trust. This experience in my own life compels me to want to share it.

Eoghan Keogh
Project Worker with Slí Eile, Jesuit Centre for Young Adults in Dublin.

Fifth Characteristic: Finding God in All Things

Towards the end of the Autobiography we read of Ignatius: "He made a solemn avowal...that his devotion, that is, his ease in finding God, was always increasing, now more than ever in his entire life. At whatever time or hour he wanted to find God, he found him" (99). Here the sixty-four year old Ignatius is speaking within a year of his death. He has come through a long process of growth that included self-knowledge, self-discipline and prayer. "Finding God in all things" is not the first step on the inner journey but the horizon that draws us onward. It is a gift given to those who persistently seek God in spirit and in truth.

A Marital Perspective on the Fifth Characteristic: Finding God in All Things

Jean and I welcomed the opportunity to reflect over the years of our marriage and finding God present there. Enough to say we have been married a long time.

We always have been, and are, endeavouring to get to know God through our couple and personal prayer. Being brought to an awareness of God's overwhelming love for us through the opening up of the Scriptures, our commitment to CLC, through listening to God's word, through reflecting on and sharing same.

Discovering how useful these skills were in relating to one another and to our children. God's grace spilling out into our family and parish and secular life; enabling us to respond to the needs of others, our involvement in our parish marriage ministry.

Being aware of the many people who have brought peace and contentment to our lives by enriching our knowledge of God as we struggled to live with the strife and conflict in our province.

Being able to reach out to the wider community.

The joy of our grand children and the boundless energy required in keeping up with them.

In our every day God can be found in the quiet, the turmoil, the joy, the sorrow, the prayer, the family, in the people we meet at work, in nature, in the world around us, in singing, in the learning to salsa and in the love we have for each other.

Jean & Peter Privilege

St. Ignatius urged his followers to: 'Pray as if everything depends upon God, work as if everything depends upon you.' For many of us, perhaps, the latter holds true, while the former doesn't even arise!

If we are to depend upon God, perhaps the first requirement is to become *aware* of him. For me, this is the key, because prayer seems to be a habit.

If we start our day *casually conversing with God* (all three of them, or any preferred one), as we dress, commute, between or on the way to engagements, we can weave that 'God awareness' into the ordinariness that is the everyday. Thus, rather than Find God in All Things through forensic spiritual searching, we can, in a more relaxed and natural way, meet him at intervals during the day through our conversations with God.

The added benefit is that when we find it hard to decide, to love, to commit, we are enwrapped in the power of his presence.

This gives us the confidence to say with the Psalmist: 'Cast your cares upon the Lord, trust in him and he will act.'

Daniel Mc Nelis
Catechist and Head of R.E. at Gonzaga College S.J.

Spiritual Exercises

There have been many references to the Spiritual Exercises in this book. Have you wondered if they might be helpful to you as you search for meaning in life? Making the Exercises is often referred to as a retreat, but it is a retreat of a particular kind. There are no talks and no devotional practices in common. Instead the focus is on allowing you, the unique individual, the space to reflect, to pray, to listen to what God may be saying in your life. An experienced guide will accompany you. Such a retreat can be as short as a weekend or as long as thirty days. It is usually made in a quiet place such as a retreat house. But the Exercises can also be made "in daily life". This means that a person continues living and working as normal but puts aside time each day for prayer. In this mode also, which can last from a week to a year, regular meetings with a spiritual guide offer the necessary support and help with discernment.

Spiritual Direction

Another resource available to anyone wishing to develop their Christian faith along the lines of Ignatian spirituality is the ministry of spiritual direction. Ignatius realised his own need to have somebody with whom he could share his inner journey and in turn became one of the great spiritual directors. He worked within a much older tradition but enriched it with his own insights. The traditional term "spiritual direction" is still widely used although some prefer alternatives such as spiritual guidance, or accompanying, or mentoring. They all point to a relationship in which one person, experienced in life and trained in the ministry, journeys with another who is searching for God in the ordinary circumstances of their life. Today this ministry is offered by priests, religious and lay people.

Further Contact

Jesuit ministries are located in Dublin, Galway, Limerick, Kildare, Belfast, Portadown and Armagh. If you would like further information and contact details, please visit the website **www.jesuit.ie**

If you want to explore the possibility of making the **Spiritual Exercises**, contact the Jesuit Centre of Spirituality, *Manresa*, on Clontarf Road, Dublin 3, **Tel: 01 8331352**, or visit their website, **www.manresa.ie**. In Limerick and Galway there are Spirituality Centres close to the schools.

If you are interested in being put in touch with a **Spiritual Director,** you can contact the Director of Manresa, **Tel: 01 8331352**, or link to the director's email on the Manresa website, **www.manresa.ie**

Further support for those working with the Jesuit ministries in Ireland – colleagues, volunteers or associates, is available from the Partners in Mission Office, contact **partners@jesuit.ie**

Other websites of interest: **www.sacredspace.ie**, a prayer website established in 1999, and 'pray as you go', **www.pray-as-you-go.org** – a British Province website offering material for downloading.

ab hiis qui rome tunc erunt convocar̃
per Literas eorum suffragia recipere͂
suffragiis eorum ut diximus qui tunc
e supradictis ad totam Societatem
poterint determinare ac si tota Societas
ac placuit et bis͂ fuit obediendo

Iñigo

Johannes Codur̃

Simon rodorici

Alphonsus salmeron

Franciscus

Edirus Jains

Ignatius

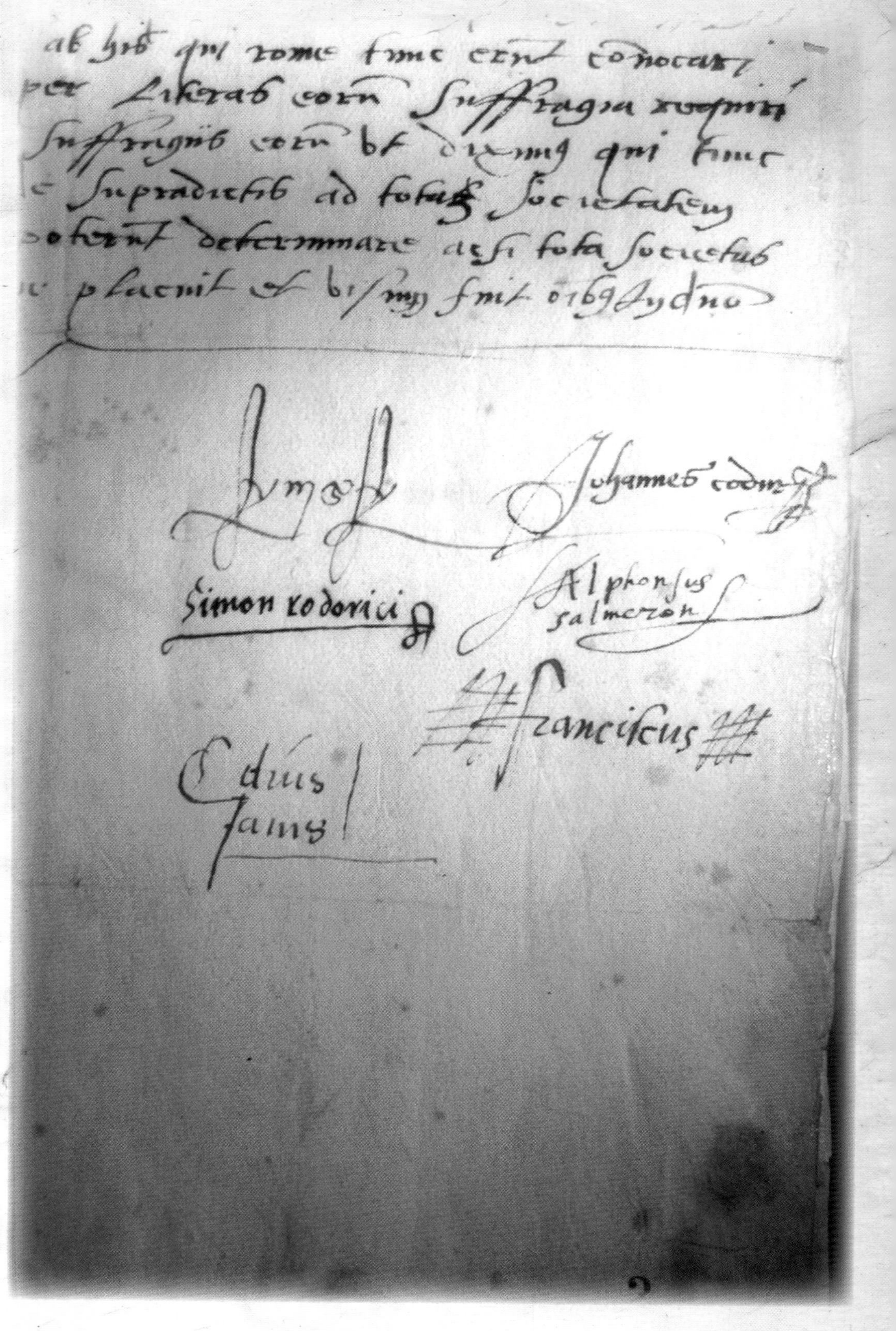